Maps and Love Songs for Mina Loy

For Neecey

Maps and Love Songs for Mina Loy

Joanne Ashcroft

Winner of the 2012 Poetry Wales
Purple Moose Prize

Seren is the book imprint of
Poetry Wales Press Ltd.
57 Nolton Street, Bridgend, Wales, CF31 3AE

www.serenbooks.com
facebook.com/SerenBooks
Twitter: @SerenBooks
www.poetrywales.co.uk
facebook.com/PoetryWales
Twitter: @PoetryWales

© Joanne Ashcroft, 2013

ISBN 978-1-78172-115-5

A CIP record for this title is available from the British Library.

All rights reserved. No part of this publication may be reproduced, stored in a retrieval system, or transmitted at any time or by any means, electronic, mechanical, photocopying, recording or otherwise without the prior permission of the copyright holder.

Printed in Plantin by Berforts Information Press

Poetry Wales gratefully acknowledges the sponsorship
of Purple Moose Brewery, Porthmadog. www.purplemoose.co.uk

Contents

Map 1	7
Map 2	8
Map 3	9
Map 4	10
Map 5	14
Map 6	15
Rose (with Mina Loy)	16
Map 8	17
Map 9	18
Map10	19
Map 11	20
Map 12	21
Map 13	22
Map 14	23
Love Songs (for Mina Loy)	24
Author Note & Acknowledgements	32

Map 1

loosely

                                      serve ink

                                                                               horny ear
                                                                             (r)amblings

                           lips scented

                            pen slivery

front row foxes chorus
                    ~/~~/~~~

deleterious   pro   gress   i   on
ssss

                                                                                         eye white
                                                                                            sight
                                                                                             trick

                              t(h)rusting

                                    signs

Map 2

spike   lick its

my love   neck

                             adorned

                             in lotions

                         girls tell

                         of

                   scattered grass

                       cut
                     eyes

                 hollow logics

                                 more tale than tease

                                                                   sins slit(her)

                soul-pocked

                                                                          cries

stall and combine

signs

yellow

enshrined

Map 3

seared with gauze
a rill safe *yawned*
armoury-ous ova

                                                                         souring spaces
                                                                          dancing dis-eased

weapon scented
foolery
of womb-i-versal-ity

                              threads croak

                            (skip li(n)es)

half alimony
minus snores

                                                                                suck
                                                                    the beautiful

                       in awe
                           I stick him
                    more tells

Map 4

torn star
sling-a-sing
pitch it harder
voice it aw(e)ful
ring old
        metallic roses
dim the sly trickle bells

                      thirty canes
                      seethe my says
                  hear sunsore earth

th'eloquent lushness
flings spring
sprints oriental
heavenly twists
sit refreshed

                    route hot tongue
                    peel paint furrows

                  free this rush higher
                    bending oxygen

with ire
land sings
flippant moanings
of limps and sores

hand back eyes
impair ear nose
ogle her lick her

fumes
thinned heart
sad sick (m)other
embers sever(e)-
ing

past her (or me)
tears sticky die and
rescind

their male-ness
hangs free on a shelf
with rude items
(eggs and gin)
      TRUTH pecks
stuns their heirloom

                    dun-one
                of chewed ear
              ponder will green
              and brew liberty

              THEN PREPARE

                                  sullenly
                                  toothsome
                                bitter grist cap
                                  it all eyes
                                scour ringing
                              count treasures on
                                        desk tiny
                              throw anchor near
                              ten souls damned
                        wrestle versed giants
                        and slide cackles at
                          you a grave away

                                        thorns gut
                                          where
                                     all guard spoils

empty ear and
pour sun where
ridge tore neck and air
Joy
surf ashes edges reef
                    re-turn her
                       love
                     grows her

Map 5

barely
        cognate
                                  a wish of asking

rose
                                                            rhymy sumpta
                                                              vestied fresh

teetered
        blue of dress
drew ties
        broad-lipped
on seas angry
rat-hacked
                                  heard her sing
pre-taleing
        hurled guilt
pen trailing
phallus
        scorned

                              talk drowned

Map 6

sever this dimple

self tune

hovver more
pry

                                                  felt his
                                      boots aped
                                        art biting
                                      actor-isms

bossoms up

sing to
the moon

                                      stick his jest
                                      lance his star

her
blushing divide
bathes her
verges
mature

Rose (with Mina Loy)

disbuddings
                                        summoning
                                   thefts of the
                                fetish
                                    in this bloodless
                                                      succour
                                        gold is dust
                                  castings
                        lapped as lupinous
                    (weeping.red.)
                          whithering greenly
                            throngings
                blue.black.white.
                        glassy
                                (the blab and the boil of it)
                        by a hook riven
                            latherings
               be-stanced
                    their arms glint of the evening sun
                              (other gods
                        foam by mouth.blister.)
                            ensouring
reigns of a disproportionate

Map 8

oval   almond
camel   kohled
red   *s(t)ings*
                a.he.fling.ing
                     his vinegar/grapes
not of
marble conch
gold   *hide*
(t)issues *observe*
succulent *guzzlings*
of sk i n f a t
an (r)etching of
     b on e s
                (dis)solving
                     in his eyes / her f(pl)ace
and *sear*-i n g
cooks it black   leathery
              oedematous
cool this
contract/ure
       SCARS/HE/R *begging*
                 for.an.end

Map 9

sprauncy
        numen sit
narcosed in
guilded smalls
           effect an
                emulgation
                      of neophiles
                                in purchasory
            ecmnesia
the imploring
milk and sugar
for t' baby bar-
            te(a)ring treats
              nepenthine drag-
              ging out of top
                to tails
                    narcohypria
                              reap of the
                              nothous
                        s(h)elling the fat-less
                                young
                            bound to
                          the visionless
                              stasis

Map 10

         rhythmic waves
     of muscular sensing eye spots
      the head generating mucus
   conceals the genital opening to
survive   hunt   and mate   thin + watery
         to edges   thick + sticky   front to back   do
eat   their own   dead   cords   lower
      not to the ground / suspend during
          copulation as self amputate i salt
             mouth-skipping   smell
          electric intestine spits
             yellow surfaces
              when ground
                  is
                 wet

Map 11

bony fronds

      tarring foil

            owl.rat.flea

                    for(m/b)idden

                    pass ages

                    insectationings

devouring fug   armpit groin

     mac/abre los ojos

corpsing memory

Map 12

in upflings of skyline
     subscapularis sinks
            sun--s--kin
            full of breathings
                  ocular waltzing
                      up pathing thighs feeling it downwards
                                           singing
            space.me.green.me.blue
w(h)ettings
     unleashings of enthrall
       foliage cantata
            bl/eaten
              flow-ridings
                    unriddled
                        heart sighs content
                                  meant being
  here   is

Map 13

                                                    spotlit snarky
                    bleeds his thrills
(this man in heels)
                      tormenting
babies strung in
diamantied dogs dancing
                    a breaking unsing
                                    --variety of formance--
titillating snouts of the eye-bound cadavers
charcoal on black
                    wallet bulging   women falling
                                      (so it says)
benumbed
     coddled
r e f l u x
                  unholied hollow smilings
                                    masks
                                            a-slipping

Map 14

      outspread
            singings
                    palpate yellowed chatterings
ensprightlied
              upcrush
                     mazing divine
                                  unfrettered
newlings
on white
          back and forth
                    all journeyings
by hand
or eye
reek
speak it down
                unbound   *unbound*
                            rise it out

Love Songs (for Mina Loy)

    I (Crib Sheet)
a. brushed post
b. person rendered
c. variously unclothed
d. sprung spring feathers   clothstains damp
e. squeak rock shake shudder lunge thrust
f. x10 a hand/mouth
g. -- 10 (10) (10) (10)
h. off-white eye morph blue
i. in a membrane his matter congealed
j. sling in a corner
k. ----
l. foil sucks
m. falls cold

I   I III IV
stopped in the mouth   litter me with
      a constellation of masterstrokes   tell
me deeper lines tilting obstructions
         graft me green a yawning eye   sown
in stickier grains heaving me sideways
   over charcoal blushes   gift it me open
luring   scaled brains akimbo   instruct me
     a smile drawn not in mockery in me un-
clothed i'll eat silent lips strobe the tongue
fasted on sunlight

V
scudding -- -- -- --
veins corroding erotic
numbing baby as guarantor / needle in
her chocolate/meat/other
presides on a bed
my unwashed -- --

VI
cover your nose to see me here
leave me here   you   seeking won't
follow

VII VIII
ultra-all I lurid in starlight
am noting
your frown spawning me un-
tempered in granite branding
that temple on
a little pink I turn

IX X XI
orbiting vacancy
        drawn in your space we
vibrate at equilibrium
        crystalline by virtue
of being tensile   we deform the wave
model of bonding

XII
loved as you I'd
not skip   ruffle
I'd cast a pastel
waltz in your dreams
with me

XIII
wrapping you
    in sucrose whispers
    nerves un-resist me fold
my tongue around your hands
-- -- -- -- -- -- -- -- -- -- -- --
all seemingly   is not   you say
I catalyst   enrupturing you
straddling entropy   mouthing
my name

XIV XV XVI
detoxic in a gown of
straw glazed pearly we
paddle the spiced foam
without wires
        naked and sated
firing collides
    pasting flesh on wheels
notched with bone

XVII
pacing I gleam a
splintered shell swinging
a lens across my belly

XVIII
deposit breath in many
cupboards for the colour of eye
in passing slits the whole

XIX
i.tri.pped.left.you.hum.ming
a.bar.mark.right.spaced
clea.ving.vi.nyl.deaf
you.too.sang.dust.lay.den
i.a.troph.y.in.my.em
et.ic

XX
farewell sweet an
ocean lips my door

XXI
stripping you out my
senses clam platinum drummed
in a lozenge of bitter rings embar-
king another sacricolist
of irregular night

XXII XXIII
heather pebbles my thigh here
lubency unbinds me   you
clover those greenments kinked by
fractured minds   encrafted   my milk seeks
a drop of grace in its teeth

XXIV XXV
too loose my hair en-
raptured you   threading we
committed a rough mecography over and
over for the feel of it   unfoolish i wept
the smog away   you played me
with flexing motions   this unhurt converted me
to you

XXV XXVI
autotoxic my body
stings a cavity   you
generate oral tentacles
to leaven it still
rigid I hang

XXVII XXVIII
briefly melichrous
       the cloche uprisen
sharp sunderings
       morsicant   adagio
i cinnabar   myrtle-less
you swaying your eyes
angel ways   re-align in
this webbed lamp

XXIX
dysphoria breeds
sucking   a high   sweeping lower
   pleasuring me bloated
      sex sore   wasted
          memory powders
   circuits upshore   births hierarchies
      etiolates my nucleus
   triggering me   lobes un-
inhibited   viscid   carving you   a tessellated
    refrain

XXX
childhood cast   torquing vistas
bickering surge in mis-
taking love   blind to us   hungered
we rebounded courting
reinforcements mochlic   un-fleshing us   those
muted gods   albicant
comp.imp.conv.ulsively we
eat a relief in sand
steel our velum
asked to   forgive   being
not ourselves

XXXI
incense sieges
you immune i hollow
my nest in riots of
ivy julep un-birthful
tumbling you bridle
your grin leaks silk-veined
swallows the moon
openly grazing i
wafer the drips

XXXII
i think not
      of you
in the body

XXXIII
your ivoried flesh nettles
me   ardent I ferment

XXXIV
aestival my love -- -- clamouring
begging unshadowed lines

Author Note and Acknowledgments

Joanne Ashcroft has had poems published in several journals. Her first book, *From Parts Becoming Whole*, was published in 2011 by The Knives, Forks, Spoons Press. She is currently undertaking a PhD researching 'Sound in the Wor(l)ds of Maggie O'Sullivan, Bill Griffiths and Geraldine Monk', at Edge Hill University, from where she has a Masters in Creative Writing.

Joanne, who lives in St. Helens, was joint winner of the Rhiannon Evans Poetry Scholarship in 2010.

The poems in this pamphlet evolved from responses to sounds created by Mina Loy in her Lunar Baedeker poems. This pamphlet is for her, with many thanks.

Some of the poems in this pamphlet were previously published in *Stride* magazine and in *em: A Review of Text and Image*.